Illustrator
Phil Hopkins

Editor
Renee Kelly, M.A.

Editorial Project Manager
Ina Massler Levin, M.A.

Editor-in-Chief
Sharon Coan, M.S. Ed.

Art Director
Elayne Roberts

Associate Designer
Denise Bauer

Cover Artists
Sue Fullam
Jose L. Tapia

Product Manager
Phil Garcia

Imaging
Alfred Lau
Ralph Olmedo, Jr.

Publisher
Mary D. Smith, M.S. Ed.

How to Make a Book Report

Grades 3-6

Author

Kathleen Christopher Null

Teacher Created Resources

Teacher Created Resources, Inc.
6421 Industry Way
Westminster, CA 92683
www.teachercreated.com
©1997 Teacher Created Resources, Inc.
Reprinted, 2005
Made in U.S.A.
ISBN-1-57690-327-3

Table of Contents

Introduction 3

Book Report Skills

Choosing a Book. 4

Writing Skills 6

Summarizing. 8

Quick Book Report Form 9

Picture Books

"Writing" the Picture Book 10

Finding Another Way to Tell the Story. 12

A Message to the Artist 14

A Picture Is Worth a Thousand Words 16

Fiction Books

Design a Book Jacket 17

Writing Journal 18

A Visit from the Character 19

Postcards from the Characters 20

Nonfiction Books

Personal Dictionary or Glossary 21

The Multimedia Book Report 22

A Book Panel 23

Spin-offs 24

Mysteries

You Read the Book; Now See the Movie! 25

Read All About It! 26

The Comic Book Version 27

A Letter from a Character. 28

Science Fiction Books

The Venn Diagram and Model 30

The Setting Haiku 31

You Are an Adventurous Traveler! 33

A Radio or Television Commercial 35

Biographies and Autobiographies

The Creative Writer 36

Make a Time Line 37

A Book Mobile and A Book Cube 38

A Scrapbook 39

Plays

My Favorite Scene 40

All About the Setting 42

A Collage 43

Setting the Scene. 44

Additional Ideas for Teachers

Having a Character Day 45

Keeping a Notebook of Book Reviews 47

Literature Journals 48

Introduction

"I want you to read this book and then write a book report." There are times when these words so discourage a student that he or she feels unmotivated to even read the book, let alone report on it. This book proves that there are many more ways to report on a book than to " . . . write a book report."

This book contains ideas for creative and enjoyable book reports in the genres of picture books, fiction, nonfiction, mysteries, science fiction, biography or autobiography, and plays. However, don't let this limit you. The ideas are creative enough to work with any genre not listed above, and very few of these book report ideas are limited to the particular genre category in which it is listed. It is highly likely that you could take a fiction book, for instance, and find a book report idea in any of these sections. Each book report idea may be copied and passed out to your students. If you wish to modify any of the ideas, it can easily be done with some correction fluid or by folding over the top section and adding your own words.

The book is divided in the following way:

★ **Book Report Skills**

This section will help your students get started. It introduces the necessary skills and knowledge your students need to create effective book reports, from choosing books to basic writing skills. Summary skills are emphasized.

★ **Picture Books**

This section contains ideas for how to report on a picture book. It includes ideas for finding ways other than writing to tell a story.

★ **Fiction Books**

This section includes a variety of activities to create reports on works of fiction. Projects including book jackets, visits from characters, journals, and postcards are found in this section.

★ **Nonfiction Books**

This section features a page of suggestions to help students create a multimedia book report. There are also ideas for a book panel, spin-offs, and creating a personal dictionary or glossary.

★ **Mysteries**

This section gives students an opportunity to participate in a newspaper activity, write a letter as one of the characters, cast a book into a movie, and create a comic strip version of a book.

★ **Science Fiction Books**

This section includes an activity in which students act as adventurous travelers preparing information about the strange and far-off places they visit when they read science fiction. It also gives them an opportunity to write haiku and a commercial.

★ **Biographies and Autobiographies**

This section contains ideas on how to do reports and projects about real people. Time lines, book mobiles, book cubes, and scrapbooks are also presented. As an extension you may want your students to write short autobiographies or, in pairs, biographies.

★ **Plays**

This sections gives ideas on how to write book reports for dramas. Here you will find information about monologues, dialogues, settings, collages and setting the scene.

★ **Additional Ideas for Teachers**

In this section you will find additional ideas for celebrating reading.

Choosing a Book

You know you need to choose a book for a book report; what do you do? Panic? Moan and groan? Run away and join the circus?

First of all, there is no need to panic if you take it one step at a time. Your teacher will probably give you a list of books to choose from, but if he or she doesn't, you can follow these steps:

1. **Think.** Start to think about what kind of book you would like to read. You might want to talk to some friends about what good books they've read recently. And don't overlook your parents and teachers. If your teacher has not given you a list, ask for one. She or he will probably be glad to give you one or show you several books to get you started.

2. **Look.** In your school or community library, there are lots of books about books. In them you can find lists of books and often information about the books. You will probably find two or three you'd like to read, and the librarian will be happy to help you find them on the shelves.

3. **Choose.** Pick two or three that seem interesting to you. Begin to read the first chapter of each to see which one you want to read first. Don't be afraid of a book with a few new words. Your vocabulary will increase, and your mind will be stretched by the experience.

4. **Give It Your All.** Don't try to get by. Read the entire book. If you try to report on a book that you have barely read, it will show, and your book report will not be as good as it could be.

5. **Record Your Thoughts.** Keep a notebook and jot down notes and quotes from the book. Write your impressions, thoughts, and feelings as you go along. Your notebook will help you later when you are ready to create your report.

Fill in the blanks below to help you decide what kind of books to choose.

These are some of the things about which I would like to know more:

animal: _____

sport: _____

hobby:_____

person: _____

time in history: _____

These are some things about which I would like to imagine:

person or creature: _____

time: _____

place: _____

fantasy:_____

someone like me: _____

If you take the two lists above to the library, the librarian can help you choose books that will interest you.

On the following page is a book wheel that you can make to help you choose a variety of books.

Choosing a Book *(cont.)*

Color and cut out the book wheel and pointer. Use a brad to attach the pointer to the center of the book wheel at the dot. Spin the pointer. Read a book from the section the arrow points to. Write the name of the book in the section, then spin again. Read again. If your pointer lands on a section you have already filled, spin again. Read at least one book from each section.

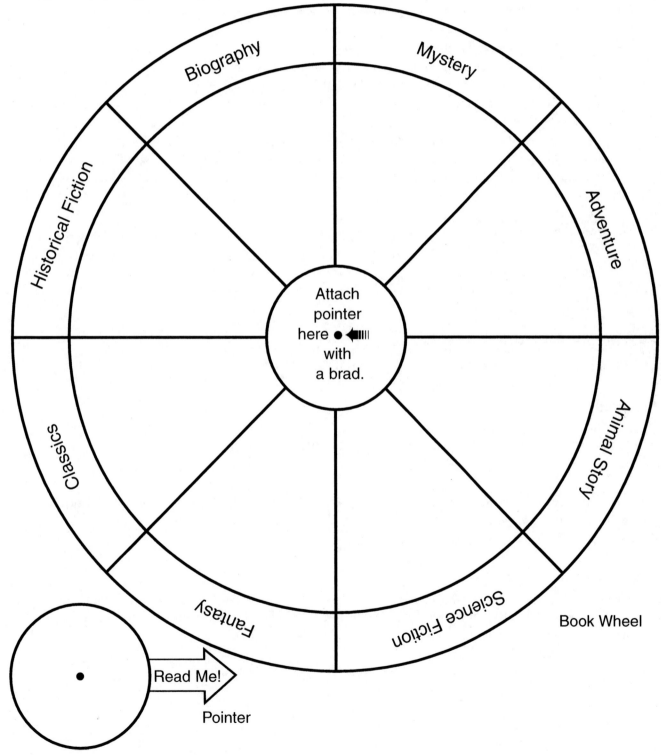

Writing Skills

The basic steps in the writing process include the following:

Prewriting
In this step you brainstorm, think about your topic, create webs and clusters, outline, research, and play around with ideas and words.

First Draft Writing
This is when you simply write all your ideas. Don't worry about spelling or grammar or anything but saying what it is that you want to say.

Revision
After you write your rough draft, go back over what you wrote. Correct spelling and grammar, look up any words you need, take some things out, add some things and arrange your paragraphs.

Evaluation
Share your work with another; it could be your teacher, a friend or parent, a classmate or others in a writer's workshop. Collect valuable information about what works and what doesn't work.

Editing and Rewriting
Now you have some fresh ideas, so go over your work again. Correct any spelling or grammatical errors you might have missed before; add any ideas you like that you got from others. Make a final copy of your story.

Publishing
When others are able to read your finished product, you have published. Your work may appear on a bulletin board, in a class book, in your own book, in a portfolio, in a newsletter, or maybe even in a magazine.

"Help!" You may be wanting to cry, "My teacher told me to write a book report. What do I do?" Just stay calm and remember that your teacher wants to know if you read and understood the book. To convince her that you did, stick with the essentials.

Evaluation
In this stage, your teacher, and/or your classmates, will let you know what they think of your report. Your teacher will evaluate your report to make sure you completed it according to the directions given to you.

Writing Skills *(cont.)*

Basic Book Report Writing Essentials

For a Work of Fiction

Title and author's name (and don't forget your own name as the author of the book report!)

Compose a theme statement. This will really impress your teacher. The theme is the main idea of the story. For instance, in the book *Charlie and the Chocolate Factory,* the theme might be that greed is ugly and unrewarded or that goodness always wins. To help you figure out what the theme is in your book, ask yourself these questions:

What does the main character learn by the end of the book?

What is the author's main purpose in writing the book? Or, if someone asked you to quickly say what the book is about, what would you say?

Summarize the story. The summary is different from the theme because in the summary you tell what happens in the story, especially what happens to the main character. Be sure you have a beginning, a middle, and an ending in your summary, just as you would in a story.

Give your opinion. End your book report by saying whether or not you like the book and whether or not you would recommend it to your friends to read.

For a Work of Nonfiction

Title, author's name and your name.

Compose a theme statement. For a non-fiction book it might be, "The author wanted to show that spiders are fascinating and not to be feared."

Summarize. Just cover the topics as listed in the table of contents. Give a few details for each, probably interesting things you learned.

State your opinion. In addition to stating whether you liked the book or not, think of the following: Did the author provide the information you expected to find? Was the writing interesting and clear? Did you learn anything new?

Summarizing

Summarizing is a special task that is not always easy to do. If your family told you to pack a small bag with only your most favorite and most important things, could you do it in one minute? Summarizing is like that. A summary includes only the most important things. In a story, whether fiction or nonfiction, you can easily figure out what the very most important things are by asking the what, who, when, where, and why questions. If you add the how question, you've got the plot. A summary needs to include some or all of the following: what it is about/what happens, who it is about/who it is, when it happens, where it happens, and why it happens. If you can, also include how it happens. For some books you may not use all of these.

Summaries are always short. They can be as short as the four or five lines you'll find describing a movie in a television listing. A summary can be one sentence, a paragraph, or a page. Your teacher can tell you just how long he or she expects the summary to be.

Here is a story pyramid that might help you to determine what the most important things are in a fiction book you have read.

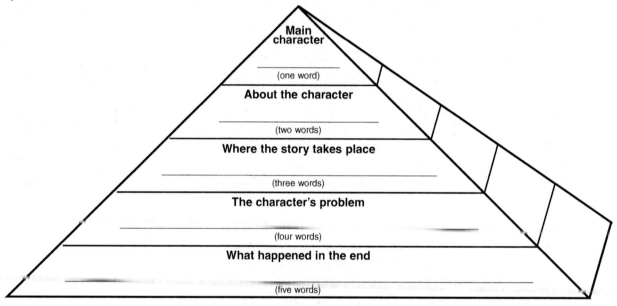

Main character
_____
(one word)
About the character
_____
(two words)
Where the story takes place
_____
(three words)
The character's problem
_____
(four words)
What happened in the end
_____
(five words)

The Summary Game

For almost any book, you can play a summary game with a friend. Here's how:

On index cards (about 5–15 of them, depending on how complicated you want the game to be), write one event per card. An event would be something that happens in the book. If your book is nonfiction, write between five and fifteen stages or topics. (For instance, if your book is about frogs, your cards will include the stages of a frog's development.)

After you write the events or stages you want to include, mix up the cards and let a friend try to put them in order. If he has not read the book, this might be very difficult for him. When he has tried his best, you can give him some clues. As you help him, you will be helping yourself remember. Writing only the most important parts of the book on index cards is a way to write a summary.

Extension: Use your cards to give an oral book report. Just put them in order and as you speak to the class, glance at your cards to remind you of what happened next. You can also use the cards to write a book report.

Quick Book Report Form

Name _____

Title of Book _____

Author _____

Illustrator _____

Number of pages _____

Type of Book (check one)
- ☐ picture book _____
- ☐ fiction _____
- ☐ nonfiction _____
- ☐ mystery _____
- ☐ science fiction _____
- ☐ biography _____
- ☐ autobiography _____
- ☐ play _____
- ☐ other _____

Fiction

The protagonist (main character or hero) of this book is_____

The antagonist or villain, if there is one, is _____

The problem the main character has is _____

He solves it by _____

Nonfiction

The main subject of this book is _____

Two things I learned are _____

_____

All books

Quick Summary: _____

_____

What I like about this book is_____

_____

What I don't like about this book is _____

_____

Why I will remember this book is _____

_____

I would/would not recommend this book because_____

_____

"Writing" the Picture Book

There are books with pictures but with very few or no words. You probably had some favorites before you could read. You used your imagination to fill in the words. You might have created your own story to go with the pictures. Picture books are fun even after we have learned how to read. The pictures tell the story beautifully. But what if we were to add words or create new words for our favorite picture books? Writing a story to go with the pictures is one way to create a book report for a picture book. Here are some ways you can do it:

- You can take your favorite picture book and write the words for each illustration on an index card. Number the cards to match the pages of the book. Then, present your book report to the class by showing the pictures while you read aloud the words you created. If your picture book has some words, cover them with a piece of paper so they don't distract you while you write or show the pictures to your class.

- Paint or draw all, or your favorite, illustrations from the book. Don't worry if your art doesn't look exactly like the artist's. In fact, if you'd like, you could create the art the way you would have done it if it had been your book. Add your own words to the bottom of each page of art. Staple your pages together or put them in a folder or notebook for the class to enjoy. You might also want to read your work to the class and show them the pictures.

- You might enjoy creating words for your book and tape-recording them. Then you can play the tape for the class while showing the pictures.

"Do you know the quickest way to town?"

- Instead of creating words of a story for your picture book, you might prefer to give an explanation of the illustrations. For each illustration, write an explanation of what is happening in the picture. Be sure to point out little details in the pictures that the class might miss. Many picture book illustrations are full of interesting or funny details.

- To make your report more challenging, you could investigate the techniques and materials that the artist used. If you can't find the information, you could ask an artist or art student to explain how the art was done. Once you know how the art was created, you can explain it to the class. And if you are feeling artistic, you can try the artist's technique yourself. Then you will have an appreciation for the artist's work. You will be able to tell the class whether it was difficult or easy to create the art.

- If simply writing the story is not enough for you, you could create a rhyming story or a poem to go with your book's illustrations.

On the following page are some examples of one student's plan to add words to a picture book.

"Writing" the Picture Book *(cont.)*

The sun was shining above the sea.

A bird flew over the waves.

He caught a fish and flew away.

The worm crawled in search of food.

Suddenly, he saw a nice, juicy leaf.

He munched happily.

Finding Another Way to Tell the Story

When you look at the pictures in a picture book, do they make you feel glad, sad, or silly? Do they ever make you laugh? Has a picture ever reminded you of some music? Here are some more ways to report on a picture book.

Music

If your picture book inspires you musically, you could create sound to go with it. If you play a musical instrument, you can record yourself playing music to go with the pictures or bring your musical instrument (or use the school's piano, if there is one) and play that music for the class. Ask your teacher how much time you should take and write about why you think the music fits the book. Or choose some music that has already been recorded. Bring a recording to class and be sure to include an explanation about how your music goes with the book.

Write a rap song to go with the pictures of your book. Be sure it is full of strong rhymes and a hard beat. Get some friends to perform it with you for a book report.

An easy way to create new music is to borrow a tune from a familiar song and write new words for it to tell the story of your picture book.

Drama

Look at the pictures. Could some of them be an interesting backdrop for a play? Write a play with two or three characters speaking to each other and acting in the setting of your book. A skit or a one-act play of one or two pages should be enough. Cast your friends in one or two of the roles, and you can take your favorite part.

Or you can write a monologue based on the pictures. A monologue is a play with just one actor (you) speaking. For instance, you might want to write a skit featuring the caterpillar from *The Very Hungry Caterpillar*. What do you think he would have to say?

Since a picture book has few or no words, a pantomime would be appropriate. To do a pantomime, you act out actions, emotions, and thoughts without any sound or words. Most pantomime artists use makeup (a white face being the most common) and costumes.

Poetry

Write a book of poetry with each illustration of the book illustrating each poem. You can choose different kinds of poetry or have the same kind of poem for each illustration. You don't need to rhyme, and you can use easy forms like anagrams for your poetry, or you can write rhyming couplets; it's your choice. Staple your poems together to make a book of your own.

If you like rhyming, you can write words to your picture book, or new words, if it already has words, and make a rhyming story. Read a couple of Dr. Seuss books to become inspired.

Finding Another Way to Tell the Story *(cont.)*

Dance

Do the illustrations in your book inspire you to leap for joy or to lumber along? Do they make you want to imitate the motions of various animals or swim through the ocean? Create some movement or dance to go with your picture book. If you wish, you can include some friends and teach them the dance. Add music, and you have an amazing book report. Be sure to ask your teacher how much time you can take for your dance before you create it.

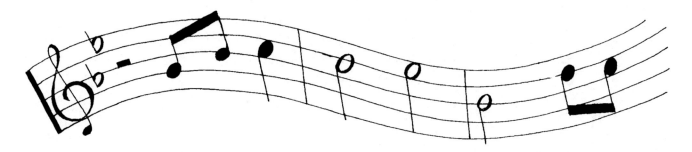

Audio/Videotape

Record a story of your picture book on audiotape to play for your class. Instead of just telling it, though, set a mood. Is it a bedtime story? Tell it with a soothing tone of voice. If it's a mysterious book full of eerie, spooky pictures, make your voice and your words as mysterious as possible.

Try a video version of your picture book. If the book is full of garden scenes, get the video camera down to stem level and move it through the grasses while you explain about the book. If you have created a written version of the book, you can read your version while you show your own video illustrations, or you might want to write and film a play based on your picture book.

A Message to the Artist

Have you ever written a letter to a book illustrator? If you haven't, you're in for a treat. Most illustrators love to hear from their readers and will write back to you (but be patient, they have busy schedules and will get to your letter as soon as they can). If you write to one and just never hear from him or her, try another. And don't worry; it's not because of anything you did; maybe the illustrator is touring the world to get new ideas and won't be back for another year.

To write to a book's artist, write the artist's name on the front of your envelope (and, of course, the top of your letter). For an address, write the address of the publishing company. This can usually be found inside the book. For example:

> Draw Well, Illustrator
> c/o Playground Publishers
> Children's Books Division
> 123 Beesknees St. #456
> Any Town, NY 10000

On the first line you write the artist's name and title (illustrator).

On the second line you write c/o, which is short for "in care of," and then the name of the company that published the book.

If the company has divisions or departments, like "Children's Books Division," put that on the third line so your letter will go to the right section of the building and reach the desk of someone who will know what to do with your letter.

On the fourth line, put the address exactly as it appears in the book.

And finally, on the last line, put the city and state, and don't forget the zip code.

The publishing company will mail your letter to the illustrator. (If you include an envelope with only the illustrator's name and a stamp on it inside the stamped envelope addressed as above, your letter will get there more quickly.)

If you have trouble finding the address, ask your teacher. You may need to look up the address in *Writer's Market*, which you can find at the library.

Write the artist to say whatever you want or to ask whatever questions you want or use the form on the next page. After you fill in the form, take an envelope and write your name and address on the front and put a stamp on it. This is called a SASE (a self-addressed, stamped envelope). If you include a SASE whenever you write to a publisher, an author, or an artist, you are much more likely to hear from them—and soon. When you hear from the artist, share the information you receive with the class for your book report.

A Message to the Artist *(cont.)*

Date_____

Dear _____

My name is _____

I am in the_____ grade at _____

I have read/looked at your picture book, _____

The thing(s) I like the best about your illustration(s) is (are) _____

I have some questions for you. Here they are.

    Can you tell me how you created the illustrations? _____

    When did you know you wanted to be an artist? _____

    Why did you decide to be an artist? _____

    How long have you been an artist?_____

    Did you study art in college or art school? _____

    What's the hardest thing about being an artist? _____

    What's the best thing?_____

    Are you working on any projects right now?_____

    What other books have you illustrated? _____

    What advice do you have for future artists? _____

Please write back as soon as you can. I will share your comments with my classmates in a special report.

Thank you very much.

Sincerely,

_____

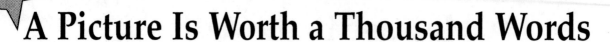

A Picture Is Worth a Thousand Words

They say that a picture is worth a thousand words. How about a picture book report from one picture? First, choose your very favorite picture from your picture book. That may be the most difficult part. Once you are sure about which is your favorite picture, you can do any of the following for a book report:

1. Recreate the picture on paper. You can do this by tracing it, drawing your own version, or making a color or black and white photocopy of the picture. Next, write a poem or haiku (see pages 31 and 32) to go with your favorite picture. Your poem doesn't have to match the book; it just needs to be inspired by the picture. Put the two together. When you make your drawing or photocopy, try to leave space for your poem somewhere on the paper, or do them separately and glue them onto a large sheet of paper.

2. Write a story that is inspired by the picture. Again, you are writing something brand new; it doesn't need to be like the book. Any story idea inspired by the picture is fine. Your story should be at least a page and a half, and if you are inspired, it can be as long as you like. Put a copy of the picture on the cover page of your story.

3. Put your picture on something else. You can put it on the front of a T-shirt, a tote bag, or apron, for instance. There are many ways to do this. Sometimes it's as easy as photocopying (if you can find a printer to do it for you). Or, trace or draw the picture on plain cotton fabric, a T-shirt, tote bag, or even the front of overalls. You can use whatever you want—transfer materials, fabric paints, or crayons. Check with your local crafts store for ideas or paint the picture onto stretched canvas, art board, or Masonite. Maybe you'd prefer to copy it onto notecards and envelopes. You are limited only by your imagination!

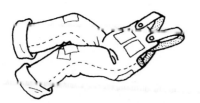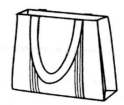

4. If you are able to collect information about how the picture was created, you can give an oral report on the art style and possibly a demonstration of the technique. You can make up a quiz to test your classmates afterwards.

5. Find other books illustrated by your picture book's artist. Check them out from the library. Compare the artist's other works to your favorite picture. Write notes about what you see. Are the illustrations similar or strikingly different from your favorite picture? Does the artist usually use the same materials and techniques, or does he or she use different materials and/or techniques? Are some pictures more or less colorful? More or less cheerful? More or less detailed or simple? Share your comparisons with the class in an oral report.

Design a Book Jacket

Do you like to read the book jacket? Do you read it before or after you read the book, while you are reading the book, or all three of the above? A book jacket is the paper cover that contains illustrations and information about the book. A book jacket has two purposes. The first is to protect the book and keep it clean and dust free, and the second, to sell the book.

You have just read a fiction book, and now it is time to sell it. You are going to inspire your classmates to read the book when they see the book jacket that you design. Here is what you will need to do:

1. With butcher paper, a brown grocery sack, or construction paper, fold a book cover for your book. You may actually make a book cover to fit, or you may simply fold a large rectangle in half and then fold the edges in about 3 inches (7.62 cm) to make the flaps.

2. On separate pieces of paper, write the "promotional text" (the information you write to inspire your classmates to want to read the book) that will appear on the flaps and on the back cover. On one flap write about what happens in the book—include something about the characters, setting, and situation without giving away the ending. On the other flap, give some information about the author. In the publishing world this writing is called the "copy" or the "blurb."

3. For the back cover, you will need to write a blurb that is so exciting that your classmates will want to read the book. It would be a good idea to use a suspenseful quote from the book that will make them want to know what happens. (Something like, "Slowly, slowly, the heavy door creaked open as she brushed aside the cobwebs, her heart pounding loudly. Then, suddenly . . . ")

4. Check your blurbs to make sure you have spelled correctly and punctuated properly. Also check to make sure that you haven't given away the story's ending.

5. If you haven't already, write your blurbs on paper that has been measured to fit the spaces on your book jacket.

6. Now you can write on the jacket itself or cut out your blurbs to paste them on the jacket.

7. Create a cover illustration. Do your best to make it interesting, attractive, colorful, or spooky, depending on what kind of book it is. Be sure to include the name of the book and its author on your cover.

8. If you have room, you can add some small drawings or borders around the blurbs on the jacket flaps. A portrait of the author on the back flap is always a good idea.

9. The back cover is probably the most challenging. Here you will have the words that will make others want to read the book. You can put background art here and then put the words on top of the art (be sure the art is not too dark) or you can draw around the words. Be sure to interest the reader, and don't give away the ending with your art!

10. Add your name to your creation and turn it in!

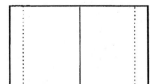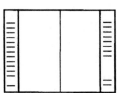

Writing Journal

A writing journal is a journal or diary that you keep while you are reading a particular book. You write entries in the journal based upon what you have read that day. When you choose one of the methods listed below, be sure to stick with it throughout your reading of that book. When you are finished with the book, you will have a completed book report!

1. Pretend that you are a character in the book. Create your journal to match the personality of that character. As the character, write in your diary each day you read, or for each chapter you read. Be sure to write in the same style in which the character speaks. Write what that character thinks about what is happening in the book and what that character thinks will happen next. Your character can also comment on the other characters in the book. Feel free to illustrate your diary.

2. Pretend you are the author of the book. At the end of each day's reading, or the end of each chapter, your author can offer commentary. An author's entry might look something like this:

   Dear Reader,

   You have probably noticed that I haven't explained everything yet. There is a reason for this, so don't get frustrated and put the book down. I haven't told you everything because I want you to discover the answers to your questions as you read the next chapters. I want you to want to read more. You are probably thinking that the house on the hill might be important. You could be right; you could be wrong. You'll just have to pay attention and keep reading. You probably noticed that I used lots of short words in the first paragraph of this chapter. I did that to make it seem like things were moving really quickly. And then, later, I took time out to describe the landscape. I hope you didn't skip that part because there are probably some clues in there, and I also wanted to slow you down some.

   Happy Reading!

3. Another way to keep a writing journal is to copy lines or paragraphs that you especially like from your reading. Write these highlights in your journal and then add your commentary. Tell why you like them, how they make you feel, and you might even add your own creative writing as you try imitating the author.

4. Maybe you would enjoy keeping a writing journal of reactions, responses, and feelings. After each chapter, take out your journal and quickly, before you forget, write your impressions. Did the chapter make you feel sad, glad, or mad? Did the chapter make you really curious and want to hurry and read the next one? Write whatever you feel, and write as much as you like. You can also add drawings to help communicate your feelings.

18

A Visit from the Character

This is a clever way to give a book report. Here is what you do to prepare:

1. Create a costume, or choose something from the closets at home, to represent a character from the book you read.

2. Write some questions to ask your character, cut the questions into strips, and put them in a small box or envelope.

3. Choose some props, if appropriate, to represent your character.

On the day of your presentation, come to class looking like the character and bring your questions and any props. Visit your classroom as if you are the character.   Speak to your classmates; tell them about your experiences in the book. When you finish speaking to your class, allow them to ask questions. If they run out of questions, you can pull out the ones that you prepared.

Here are some sample questions which you can use for yourself, or give copies of this list to your classmates to help them come up with questions to ask you.

- What is your name?
- How were you named?
- What book are you from?
- Who wrote the book?
- How is your story told? (Is the book funny? Scary? Serious?)
- How do you act in the book?
- Why do you look like that (costume, etc.)?
- Did you enjoy the book you were in? Why?
- Did you have a favorite character in the book? Why?
- Did you like the way the book ended? If not, how would you change it? Why?
- What is your favorite color?
- What is your favorite food?
- What do you like to do?
- Where do you like to go?
- What would you like to have happen in your next book? Why?
- Where do you live?
- Do you go to school? Where?
- Who is your best friend? What do you like to do together?
- If you are not grown up yet, what do you want to be when you grow up?
- If you are grown up, what did you want to be when you were little?
- What do you think of our school?
- What do you think of our city/town?
- Now that you are visiting us, what do you want to do or see?

Postcards from the Characters

Fill in this postcard for your book report. Pretend a character in your story is writing you a postcard.

Directions:

1. Cut out the postcard.

2. Write what the character might tell you.

3. Address it to yourself.

4. On the back, draw a picture of the place from where that character is writing to you.

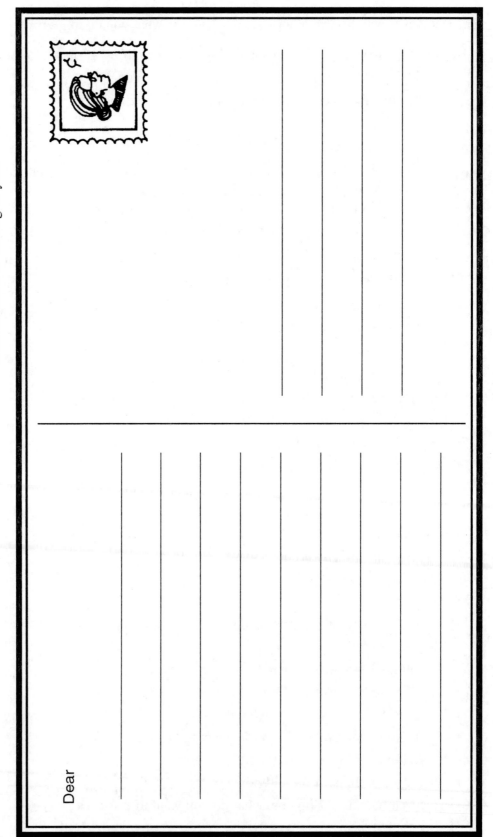

Dear _____

20

Personal Dictionary or Glossary

You're learning new words all the time, especially when you are reading. Your vocabulary will increase significantly if you try a system for remembering the new words that you come across in your reading. And the system can also work as a book report.

When you pick out your book, also pick out, or make, a notebook to go with the book. Put the title of the book on the cover of your notebook, along with the words "Dictionary," "Glossary," or something like "Interesting Words," and divide your notebook into sections or chapters to match those of the book.

As you read, keep your notebook nearby. When you come to an interesting or new word, jot it down in your notebook. You can add words that are not new to you but that you want to know more about, such as how the word originated or other meanings that you may not have known.

When you write the word in your notebook, include the sentence in which the word appears. It's important to know how to use a word, and the context (the words around the new word) contains important clues.

- Include your guess as to what the word means. It's fun to see if you were right, close, or completely wrong.
- Look up your words and write their definitions in your notebook.
- Highlight or circle the definition that matches the meaning of the word from your book.
- Add pictures to your book to illustrate the words or the parts of the book from which the word comes.
- You can also add your personal commentaries such as:

"I like this word because . . ."

"This word has special meaning to me because . . ."

"This word reminds me of another word . . ."

"When I looked up I saw the usual migratory geese, honking and hurrying in their inverted V-shapes, only this time I felt as if I was the one being left behind."

migratory

1. the act of migrating 2. a group of people, or birds, fishes, etc., migrating together

The book talks about migratory geese, so now I understand why they're flying together in the same direction. But I never heard of migratory people. I wonder who they might be.

"To walk from the door to her bunk beds, I had to get through a labyrinth of books, games, magazines, and tapes."

labyrinth

1. a structure containing an intricate network of winding passages hard to follow without losing one's way; maze.

At first I didn't get this. I thought I might have to look it up in another dictionary. But after I thought about it, I could picture a messy room being like a maze where a person could get lost.

The Multimedia Book Report

If your school has a computer with a multimedia program, you can take your nonfiction book and create a demonstration for your classmates.

Computer Multimedia

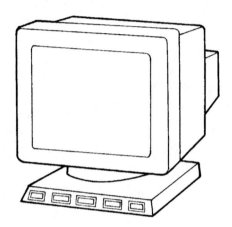

Think about what you learned and what you can teach to others. Make a list. Next divide your subject list into four or five sections. Put one section on each card in the stack. If you need help in using multimedia, your teacher can help, or you can use the book that comes with the program. When your stack is completed, run through it to see if it's the way you want it. You can change things if you want. If your program allows the use of sound and video, you can add that by creating your own sounds and videos, using those available in the program, or borrowing some from a CD encyclopedia. When you are finished, your classmates can explore the topics to be found in the book you read. Be sure to include your opinion of the book somewhere in your report.

Video

You can create a documentary about your book and its subject. Before you begin, it might help if you can view a documentary. Ask your teacher or a parent to help you find one. Public television will usually have a selection. Watch to see the many ways that information is presented: visually, musically, quotes, stills, background information, etc. Collect as much material, both written and visual, as you can. If your book is about a famous artist, for example, you could videotape several of the paintings (copies, posters, in books, etc.) to music. You could read quotes from the artist while videotaping an easel, a still life, or a landscape. You could videotape yourself, seated at a desk, telling an interesting story about the artist and showing some examples of his or her work.

Interaction

Involve your classmates in your learning by creating games that present the things you learned from your book. You might want to use a game after you have presented your information with one of the above methods, just to be fair. A crossword or word search puzzle might challenge your classmates. A board game might be even more impressive. Create a board game on a folding file folder and have your students move game pieces around the board by answering questions correctly.

Slide Show

If you like photography, you can take slides to represent the subject of your book. When you get your slides back, arrange them in a slide show and add music and words to go with them. Present your show to the class.

A Book Panel

If several of you have read the same nonfiction book, you can present a panel of experts. You and two to five other students can brainstorm to come up with what you think are the three to six most important topics of the book that you read. For instance, if you read a book on dolphins, your topics might be their habitat, their diet, their history, their family life, and kinds of dolphins, and where they can be found in the world.

Next, each of you on the panel will need to take one topic. You will each become an expert on your topic.

To become an expert, look through the book you read and find everything you can on your topic. Use index cards to take notes. In addition, find visual aids (pictures, graphs, maps, charts) and make large copies of them.

Go to the library to find additional information to fill in what you don't already know.

Once you have become an expert on your topic, take your index cards and write a one-page report that summarizes what you know. In this report you don't want to give every detail, just the main facts. Hold on to your index cards for the details. If you want, you can write a list with a paragraph of information for each item.

Get together with the other panel members to share your information. You want to be sure that you don't have the same information that another panel member plans to use.

Read your reports aloud to each other and get feedback on such things as, "Is my report clear? Is it interesting?"

Choose a panel leader to act as the spokesperson for the group.

Make any necessary revisions and arrange your index cards so they are in the same order as your report.

Now your panel is ready. On the appointed day, you will all go to the front of the classroom and sit at a table or two.

First, you will introduce your topic and read your summaries. For example, have the spokesperson say something like this:

"We have each read *The Dolphin Book* by Juliette Seaweed and we have become experts on dolphins. First we will hear from Nick, who will present his topic, the dolphin's habitat. Next we will hear from Mio who will be reporting on the dolphin's diet. Then we will hear from . . . ," etc.

After each panel member has presented a summary, it is time to open up the panel for questions. As the questions are asked, the person who is the expert on the topic is the one to answer the question. This is where good index cards will come in handy.

If you are asked a question and don't know the answer, it can be asked of anyone on the panel. If no one on the panel knows the answer and if the rest of the students and the teacher don't know the answer, the question should be written down and the panel member who is the expert on the topic can find the answer and bring it to class.

Spin-offs

Imagine that your favorite television show is about aliens living on a farm in the country. The show is so popular that other shows, called spin-offs, are created, such as a show about the alien children growing up and going to college in the city. A spin-off is something related to the original topic with enough interest to be its own "show." So, if you read a book about Japanese baseball, the spin offs might be the history of Japan, the food of Japan, the music of Japan, the Japanese language, the Japanese people, baseball in other countries, the history of baseball, etc. Are you getting the idea? To get you thinking, fill in the blanks below:

My nonfiction book's title is_____

The author is _____

The main topic of the book is_____

_____

The subtopics and related topics are_____

_____

Now that you've come this far, take out a sheet of paper and draw a line down the middle to divide your paper in half lengthwise. You will be brainstorming, so if you think you'd like more room, use two pieces of paper side by side. List on the left side of the paper every topic you can think of that is related to your main topic. In the right-hand column (or on the next piece of paper), list every category you can think of such as food/cooking, customs, geography, history, folklore, stories/myths, etc.

Now look at your list, and circle any connections you can find (such as whaling: history, geography, and folklore).

Next, think of how to best present your spin-off. If you will be presenting the foods of Africa, for instance, you could do a cooking demonstration or bring samples and a recipe booklet to class to pass out to your classmates. Be sure to be prepared to explain your presentation's connection to the nonfiction book you read. If you read a book about the Vietnam War, you could do a spin-off presentation of the music of the period or Vietnamese food or culture, etc. If you read a book about volcanoes, you could demonstrate a volcano, but you could also create a relief globe showing where all the volcanoes are located or give a presentation on the geography of Hawaii or Italy (and some Hawaiian or Italian food might not be a bad idea, either).

A book about fabric design could spin-off a demonstration of batik or tie-dye or the history of early fabric art, India, Indonesia, etc. A photography book might spin off an activity in photo-collage with your classmates creating art under your direction. If you read a book about dogs, you might be able to demonstrate dog training techniques or give a presentation about police dogs or other working dogs. A book about Ireland or an Irish person could inspire Irish dance, Irish music, Irish history, or Irish food.

You Read the Book; Now See the Movie!

While you were reading your mystery, you might have thought about how it would make a good movie. Maybe your imagination was like a movie in your head. Here is your chance to use your imagination to help promote the movie. Imagine that the directors, producers, and writers have met together and have decided to make your mystery into a movie. Your job is to cast the actors, create the movie posters, and write the synopsis.

Casting the Actors

First, write a characterization of each of the most important characters in the book. A characterization is a character description. You will need this to help you to cast the actors and actresses. Here are some sample characterizations: "Damion—tall, dark, and moody; often seen walking about in the fog wearing a long, dark cape; keeps to himself and rarely smiles." "Laura—sweet and plain, wears thin, flowered dresses; often seen carrying her cat; young and pale." Next, list the most important characters, leaving a space after each name. Think about what actor or actress would seem right for each role and write his or her name in the appropriate space.

Create the Movie Posters

Use two large sheets of poster board. With paints, markers, and/or crayons, create two posters advertising the movie. You might want to have two different suspenseful scenes in the background and, depending on how many characters, one or two different actors on each poster. Your poster should feature the name of the book (also the name of the movie) in bold letters. Include the names of the actors and the author of the book. Add your name as one of the producers.

Write a Synopsis

A synopsis is a very short summary of the movie. To become familiar with what a synopsis is, look at television and movie listings. In a very short paragraph, they tell what the program or movie is about. Often you can find a synopsis on a book jacket, as well. A synopsis sounds something like this:

"Laura thought it would be a dull summer until the new family moved in next door. When the weather became strange and the neighborhood cats began to walk down the street together every afternoon at 3 p.m., Laura knew it had something to do with the new neighbors. Laura spends the rest of the summer investigating, with her friends, the mystery on Tulip Lane."

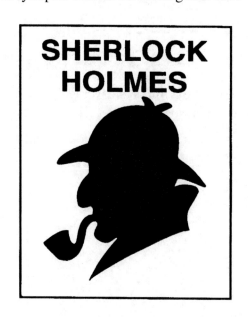

When your two posters are completed, bring them, your characterizations, your casting list, and synopsis to school to share with your classmates.

Read All About It!

If you pick up a newspaper you will find it full of mysteries. What better way to report on the mystery you read than to present it as the headline news. You are the expert on your subject, so you will be the newspaper editor. You can also be the newswriter, photographer, and reporter. If several of you read the same mystery and your teacher has encouraged you to do a group project, you can each take a position in creating your newspaper.

The simplest way to create your newspaper would be to use newspaper-size sheets of butcher paper. You can type or handwrite your headlines and stories and glue them into place on the paper.

Headlines need to be short, big, and bold, and they need to catch the eye of the reader. Here is a sample headline that doesn't do those things:

Mayor of Dryridge Gulch Has a Meeting With Residents of the East Side of Town About Recent Events

Here is a better headline:

Mayor Meets with Witnesses About Mysteries of East Side

The photographs can be drawings with captions glued into place. If you wish, you can get your friends to pose and take black and white photographs and glue them into place.

Captions are one or two lines that are placed just below photographs or drawings. They need to tell who and what is in the picture. For example:

From left to right, Jordan and Missy Stewart, Lisa Gomez, and Ralph the dog, point out the mysterious markings they found in Richard's field.

If you want more of a challenge, and you have access to enough technology, you can use a print program's newsletter section to create a computer generated newspaper. Use scanned photos, if possible, or use the computer's draw program to create your own drawn "photographs."

In the text of your newspaper articles, be sure to include all the pertinent information: who, what, when, where, and why. One article might cover the mysterious setting (where). Several articles might cover the people involved (who). The lead article, the one with the biggest headline, might best be reserved for what happened and when. Since your book is a mystery, be careful when you write an article to tell why. You might want to eliminate coverage of the "why." Only include it if you can do it in a mysterious way without giving away the ending. Now that would be a challenge to any newspaper writer!

Include a short article about the book's author and be sure to give yourself credit as the editor, writer, photographer, etc.

The Comic Book Version

Comic books are fun to read, and they're also fun to create. This could be an especially enjoyable way to report on a book.

1. Use two copies of the form below for your book report. The first strip is for planning. The second one is for your final project.

2. Choose an important scene from your book which involves two or more characters. Read the scene again while taking notes on the setting or place, the characters involved in the action, and any ideas you think might be expressed in this scene. Also, note any important details: how a character is dressed, what a character is carrying, etc.

3. On the rough draft copy, sketch your ideas. You probably won't be able to get all the dialogue you want into your strip, so shorten it to the most important words.

4. When you have it the way you want it, create your final copy in ink or markers. Be prepared to explain why you chose the scene you did, the importance of the details, etc.

Name _____

Title of Book _____

Author _____

A Letter from a Character

As you read your mystery, did you ever wonder what a character would tell you about the story if he or she had a chance? Maybe an antagonist (another name for a villain or any character who creates obstacles or difficulties for the main character) would like an opportunity to explain his or her side of the story to you. Here is your opportunity to use your imagination and write a letter from a character in the book to you, the reader.

First, choose a character. The main character, or protagonist, may have already had his story told to his satisfaction, so you may want to look at other characters.

Next, make a list of the things this character would probably want to include in a letter to you.

Then, create a letterhead for your character (see examples on page 29). Be creative and think of your character's traits as you create the letterhead. Would the art and lettering look innocent and sweet or dark and dastardly?

And finally, write the letter. Be sure you stay in character and write just as the character speaks. If the character tends to be a pessimist or an optimist, write grumpily or cheerfully.

Be sure your name is at the top where it says, "Dear . . . ," and have the character sign his or her name at the bottom.

If you'd like, you can have your character insert an extra sheet of paper to draw diagrams or illustrations of what it is he or she is trying to explain to you or include a scene from the book.

Here is an example of a character's letter:

Dear Ryan,

Now that you've finished reading *Megan's Ghost*, I would like to explain a few things to you.

First of all, it really isn't fair that everyone thought I was a mean person. I was only trying to keep my promise to Megan. She had come to me when I was just a little girl and asked me to keep her secret. All my life I have kept her secret.

When that family moved in and those children, Timothy and Hannah, started to snoop around, I had no choice but to do things to try to keep them from discovering the secret. I didn't dislike the children. I just had to keep my promise.

It also wasn't fair that Megan changed her mind as she did. She could have told me. I could have been helpful.

Instead, everything got more complicated, and it was harder and harder for me to keep my promise.

Now that everyone knows about Megan's ghost, I don't have to keep my promise anymore. It would nice if someone could thank me for trying so hard to keep my promise all those years.

It's really not fair.

Sincerely,

Adelle

A Letter from a Character *(cont.)*

Below are some examples of stationery to give you some ideas about how to design the stationery or letterhead for your character:

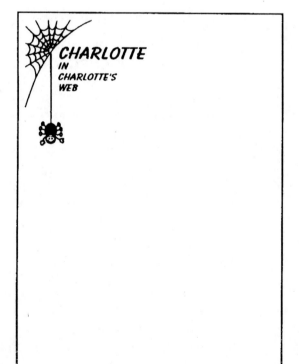

The Venn Diagram and Model

A Venn diagram is one way to report on a book. A Venn diagram based on a science fiction book can be especially interesting.

First, decide what two things you will want to compare. You may want to compare two characters in the book, or two settings: the science fiction setting and your own. Or you may want to compare a character in the book to yourself. Here is an example of a Venn diagram comparing a science fiction character to the reader:

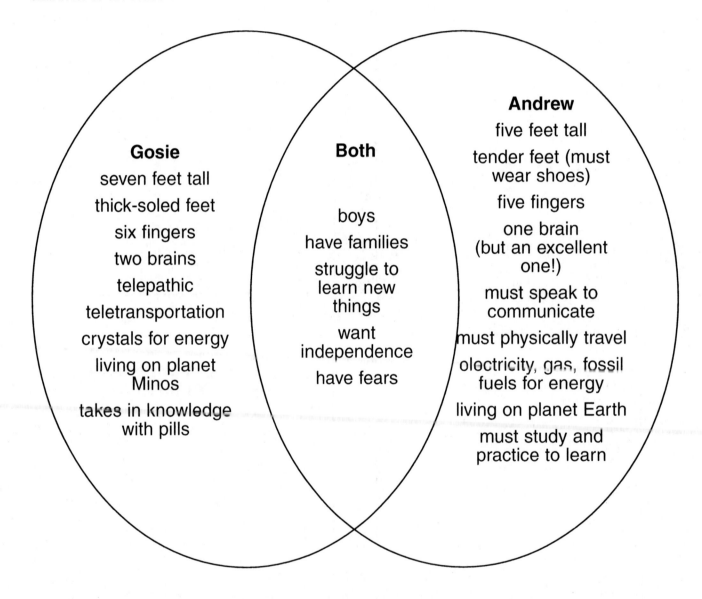

Gosie

seven feet tall

thick-soled feet

six fingers

two brains

telepathic

teletransportation

crystals for energy

living on planet Minos

takes in knowledge with pills

Both

boys

have families

struggle to learn new things

want independence

have fears

Andrew

five feet tall

tender feet (must wear shoes)

five fingers

one brain (but an excellent one!)

must speak to communicate

must physically travel

electricity, gas, fossil fuels for energy

living on planet Earth

must study and practice to learn

Now that you have compared your character to yourself, create a model of your character. Using play clay from a toy store, in lots of different colors, create the character from your book. Or mix up your own play clay and use food coloring to make different colors. If you prefer, you can use plain clay and paint it after it dries with acrylic paints. Include all the details that make him or her so different from you. When your model has dried, bring it and your Venn diagram to class as your book report.

The Setting Haiku

How would you like to be able to write a book report in just three short lines? Does it sound like a dream come true? Before you get too excited and decide that this is the book report for you because it will be easy, give it some thought. That is exactly what this book report will require: careful thought. In this book report you will describe the setting of your story with a haiku and an illustration.

First, think about the setting of your book. How do you see it? Does it take place at a space station in the stars? another planet? Go back and look in your book for descriptions of the setting. Write some notes and brainstorm. List some of the items and what they look like. One student listed for her setting: magnetized travel pods, large crystals, a desert-like planet, two suns, hot temperatures on the planet's surface, cool underground, gray concrete maze-like tunnels.

Next, draw your setting. Include as many things from your list as you can.

Now write a haiku. Haiku is a form of Japanese poetry. It has three lines. The first and last lines have just five syllables and no more. The second line has seven syllables. Haiku requires thought because each word is important in describing the mood or feeling of a scene or setting. A haiku usually focuses on just one or two images that suggest a time of day, a season, a physical place, or what is special about something in nature. The haiku writer focuses on the senses and what the setting means to him or her. Here is a typical haiku:

> *Dolphins in the waves,*
> *Sliding down the sloping sea;*
> *I join with my eyes.*

The haiku above is typical because it is about a setting in nature, and it indicates the writer's response. Here are some haikus based on book settings:

> *Winter light sparkles*   *Solid wood beneath*
> *Coating all the prairie sod*   *Swirling winds torment above*
> *With sparkling sprinkles*   *Only safe right here*

The first was written by a student who read one of Laura Ingalls Wilder's books. The haiku describes a winter scene from one of the chapters. Notice all the "s" sounds she used? Repetitive use of a sound is a poetic tool known as *alliteration*. The second haiku is by a student who read a book about some boys who survived a storm in a treehouse fort.

Here is the haiku written by the girl who brainstormed above (compare her brainstormed list with her haiku):

> *Crystals, magnets zoom*
> *Cool wind whooshing through gray tubes*
> *Leaving heat above.*

The Setting Haiku *(cont.)*

Now you have the challenge of taking a scene from your science fiction book and writing a haiku to describe the setting. The only rule is to keep your lines to the pattern of five, seven, and five syllables. Write several rough drafts before you come to the words you like the best. Don't be discouraged if you write many drafts. It would be better for you to write many drafts and find one you really like than to write one or two drafts and turn in one that you feel is just "okay." Use the lines below to write your drafts. When you have one you like, write it carefully at the bottom of your paper. Add your illustration above your haiku. There, you've accomplished something special!

_____

_____

_____

_____

_____

_____

_____

_____

Extension: If you decide you like writing haikus or if you wrote several that you like and can't decide which one to use for your book report, use several! Staple them together or place them in a report folder. Don't forget to add additional illustrations.

Write one or two paragraphs telling how you chose the words you used in your haiku. What are you describing? What is important about it? What is happening? etc.

_____

_____

_____

_____

_____

_____

_____

_____

You Are an Adventurous Traveler!

When you read a science fiction book, you travel to new frontiers. You become a kind of pioneer or scout to your classmates who have not read the book that you read. Let's say you read a book that has as its setting the planet Cyphera. By the time you have finished reading, you know all about the planet, its weather, the people there, their customs and government, and what is worth seeing.

Imagine that you have been chosen to represent a travel agency and share your knowledge with the public. The travel agency has asked you to prepare a travel brochure, a poster, and a map for those who would like to know what to expect when they travel to Cyphera. (Note: You may wish to visit a travel agency to look at travel brochures and posters. You can probably take some home as examples.)

Travel Brochure: Take a large sheet of white (or any color that is pale enough for your writing to be clear) paper. Fold horizontally in thirds (accordion style or with two outside flaps folding inward). You now have six rectangular panels to work with. On another piece of paper, brainstorm for topics to put on each panel. You may come up with five topics or more (put two topics on one panel if they are related and short enough). Some topics you may wish to include are the weather on Cyphera (when to go, what to pack), the food (what to be sure to try, what to avoid), the culture and customs of the people (maybe on Cyphera it would be a bad idea to wave; it may have a different meaning there; there may be some strange customs that need explaining), the economy—shopping, paying for items and services— the government and history of Cyphera (tourists may need to know if they are to bow to the leader of the planet each day at a particular time), transportation (how to operate the magnetic hovercrafts), the hours in a day on the planet, etc. On the front panel of your brochure, draw a picture that will entice the tourists. If Cyphera is especially beautiful from space, draw it from that view. If it has some interesting plants or buildings, draw those. Add the name of the planet with a slogan, maybe something like "Cyphera, the cool blue planet. Once you arrive, you won't want to leave!" At the bottom of this first panel, put the name of the book, its author, and your name. You can add a title to your name, such as "Travel Scout" or "Adventurer." Use the remaining panels for your important information about the travel destination. Add illustrations wherever you like.

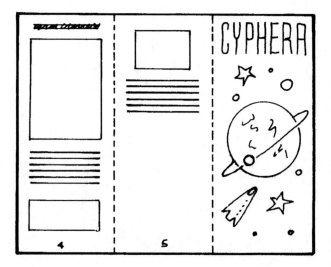

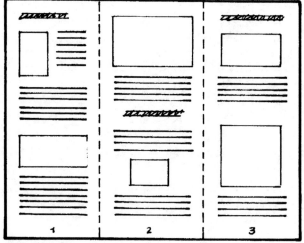

You Are an Adventurous Traveler! *(cont.)*

Poster: On poster board, create a large poster illustrating your travel destination. In the case of Cyphera, there may be a drawing of the planet as one might see it when approaching it from space, or there may be a picture of the people, Cypherians, greeting visitors. And of course, there will be the name of the destination and an enticing line or two welcoming the tourists. Sketch your ideas on paper before putting them on the poster board. Use bright colors on the final product.

Map: From your reading, make a sketch of where you think various landmarks would be found. On a large sheet of paper, draw a map to direct visitors to the various locations. Use color and detail to make your map interesting and be sure to create a key for your map. For a key, draw a box and within it place the symbols that you wish to use on your map to indicate such things as transportation routes, important buildings and landmarks, and various terrains such as mountains, deserts, lakes, or craters.

34

A Radio or Television Commercial

You are trying to sell the book you have just read. You would like everyone you know to buy it for a birthday present for someone they know. How would you sell your classmates the book? How could you make them want to buy it? Fill in the blanks below, and then write your television or radio commercial. When you have practiced what you wrote, present your commercial to the class.

Title of book:_____

Author: _____

Price of book: _____   Pages: _____

Why everyone should read this book: _____

_____

The most exciting part of the book (Don't give away the ending!): _____

_____

Why this book will make a great gift: _____

_____

Use this form to create your own.

My commercial for: _____

I think everyone should buy at least one copy of this book and read it because_____

_____

_____

This book will make a great gift because _____

_____

Buy it today! It is only $ _____ . You couldn't buy a better gift!

Extension: Tape-record your radio commercial. Create a radio program and let it be sponsored by your commercial or make a videotape of your television commercial. Have a friend or parent film you. Be creative, use props (at least the book, but you could also make yourself look like a character in the book, use science fiction-type props that you have made, etc.) and a colorful but uncomplicated background (could even look like a setting in the book).

The Creative Writer

A biography or autobiography is a book written about the life of a person. It is a true story based on facts, and so it is nonfiction. A biography is a book written by an author about another person. An autobiography is a book about a person by the same person. So, if you write a book about President Lincoln, you are writing a biography. But if you write a book about yourself, you are writing an autobiography. If you go to the library and look in the biography section, you will probably be surprised to see how many books there are about famous and not-so-famous people. Check some out and read one. When you finish, you can use your creative writing skills to write a unique book report. The biography or autobiography you read is nonfiction, but you can write a book report using formats that are often considered to be more suitable for fiction: poetry, vignettes, or skits.

Poetry: Write a poem about the subject of your book. Your poem can rhyme at every line, at every other line, or not rhyme at all. It can also be an acrostic or haiku. Using the Abraham Lincoln example from above, some poems might look like this:

Loved Freedom
Investigated slavery
Never gave up
Communicated well
Ordered that slaves should be freed
Liberty for all
Name will always be remembered by all

Lincoln was so very tall
And brave and kind and true.
He spoke of freedom for us all,
For some his words were new.

The tall, dark man sat deep in thought
His troubled mind did cease to rest
He thought of those, unfairly kept
Those kept from freedom, those oppressed.
He bent beneath his load of care
His country's war did pierce his breast,
And drove him ever on to seek
Solution to his noble quest.

Vignette: A vignette is a short (usually one paragraph to two pages) piece of writing that is sometimes called "a slice of life." A vignette takes a day or an hour and describes everything about that day or hour: the setting, the people, the senses, the mood, all that can be seen in that little space. A vignette is also sometimes known as a "snapshot." To write a vignette about the subject of your biography or autobiography, pick a day or small amount of time from his or her life. Describe it in great detail. Perhaps he or she is at the beach with his or her parents when young. What are they doing? Is there the sound of seagulls and crashing waves? What do they say to each other? Remember to include a description of the setting and use as many of the senses as you can.

Skit: Using an episode from the life of the person you have read about, write a short skit to illustrate what you learned. You can make it a one-person skit, or you can recruit one or two friends to play other roles. Time your skit to be 2–5 minutes long. Add props and anything else that will enhance your skit. It can be funny or serious, but be prepared to explain why you chose what scene you did.

Make a Time Line

Each of us lives our lives during some unique period of history. You have probably wondered what your life would be like if you had been born at a different time. What would your life be like if you had been born long before automobiles, airplanes, television, and computers? When we read biographies and autobiographies, we are often given a glimpse into other times and other places.

You will be creating a time line that shows the life span of the subject of your biography or auto-biography. The first thing you will need to do is to find out the subject's birth date and year. Then you will need the date of his or her death. If he or she is still alive, your time line will go to the present day.

Use your two dates to do your research. For instance, if your subject lived in the United States between the years of 1835 and 1898, you will want to look up some books and computer encyclopedia information on what was going on in the United States for the 63 years between those two years. Perhaps your subject lived in Scotland in the 1700s or Africa from 1950 to the present. There are many books and encyclopedias that feature time lines, so you can use that information.

In addition to what information you collect about what was going on in the country during the subject's lifetime, you will also need to collect information about what was going on in his or her own life. Jot down events and arrange them in chronological order (the order in which they happened).

Now you are ready to make your time line. Measure out about four or five feet of butcher paper and draw a line down the length of it, dividing the paper in half lengthwise. A yardstick can help you make a straight line. Mark the years along that line. With another color, mark the places on the time line when events occurred in the life of your subject. Below the line, write what happened when and anything else that is important as room allows. You can add photocopied pictures or draw pictures to illustrate some or all of the events. With another color, mark important events in U.S. history. Above the line, write about the events and include pictures. If you have a computer, you can use a software program titled *Timeliner (*Tom Snyder Productions) to assist you in creating a time line.

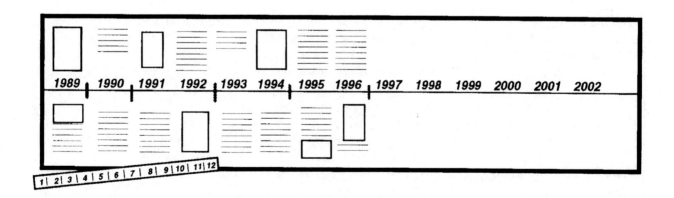

When you have completed your time line, and can stand back and look at it, you will see how the subject of your book fits in with history. You may want to read the book again!

Extension: If the subject of your book lived during your lifetime, add your own life to the time line in yet another color or create your own time line to compare your life with your country's history.

A Book Mobile and A Book Cube

Mobiles are fun and cubes are interesting. You could make one or both for the biography or autobiography you have read.

Book Mobile

You will need the following:

- construction paper shapes (squares, rectangles, circles, triangles)
- white drawing paper
- yarn
- cardboard tube (paper towel or giftwrap)
- scissors
- glue
- crayons or markers

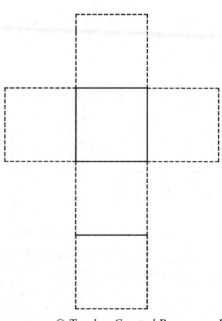

Directions:

1. Draw the people and the events from the book on the white paper. Color your pictures.
2. Cut out your pictures and glue them to the construction paper shapes.
3. Punch a hole at the top of each shape.
4. Tie a piece of yarn to each one.
5. Make four slits in the cardboard tube as illustrated.
6. Force the yarn through the slit and secure it with a knot.
7. Hang your mobile by another length of yarn tied at the center.

Book Cube

You will need the following:

- markers, pens, pencils
- glue or transparent tape
- pattern (enlarged)

Directions:

1. Decide how you will use the six squares of the cube. Brainstorm and choose your six favorite ideas. Each cube could represent an event or stage in the life of your subject or you could use four or five squares for events or stages and one or two squares to write about the subject and the book and its author. For instance, if your book is about Thomas Edison, you might use a square to draw a picture from his childhood, one to show him inventing the light bulb, etc.
2. Fill in the six squares with the artwork and writing that you have chosen. Be sure to be colorful and write neatly.
3. Cut out the cube along the dashed lines. Fold. Glue or tape along the bold lines.
4. Display your cube!

A Scrapbook

Do you have any scrapbooks at home? Ask a parent to show you one. If you don't have one, a relative or friend may have one. A scrapbook is a book full of memories. In a scrapbook you will find pictures, cards, ticket stubs, programs, awards, locks of hair, recipes, invitations, birth announcements, holiday cards, pressed flowers, scraps of fabric, letters, notes, etc. Usually a scrapbook is full of the memories of one person. For a book report, you can make a pretend scrapbook for the person you just read about in a biography of autobiography. Here's how:

- Begin by purchasing a scrapbook or make one with large sheets of construction paper or butcher paper. Make a cardboard cover to fit.

- Decorate the cover and add the name of the subject of your book.

- Put your name at the bottom.

- Brainstorm a list of everything you can think of about the subject of your book: everything he or she did, liked, wanted, tried, said, thought, loved, etc.

- From that list, brainstorm everything you can think of that your subject might have around in his or her personal things as mementos or just clutter.

The following information will give you ideas about what to collect and make.

Collect and make items that might go into the scrapbook: if your subject has red hair, you might add a snip of red hair (ask before you snip of course!); if your subject is an athlete or any kind of famous person, create a newspaper article about him or her and glue it to a scrapbook page; create a birth announcement for your subject to glue into the scrapbook; you can also add photocopied pictures of the subject and his or her family.

There is no end to the items you can create from your subject's memories. You can write a letter in your subject's handwriting (however you think it would look). If the letter should look very old or as if it came from a battlefront, you can crinkle it, rub it, and paint it yellow around the edges. If your subject was on the stage, you can add a ticket stub and a piece of fabric that looks like it could have come from his or her costume. If your subject is a musician, you can add guitar stings, sheet music, or a reed. If your subject ran for office, design a ballot with his or her name on it, along with the other candidates, and design a campaign button if you can't find the real one. If your subject was an inventor, create some notes; an artist, some sketches. Don't forget awards, ribbons, special letters from others, and letters and drawings from your subject's family members and friends. You might even want to create a report card for when your subject was your age.

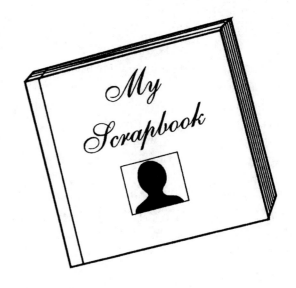

Now, take out a piece of paper and start brainstorming!

My Favorite Scene

Do you ever watch a movie and want to tell your friends about a scene that is your favorite part? A play is like a movie. It was written to be acted by actors. We also read plays, though, because our imaginations let us see the actors acting in our minds. In the play you have read, there is probably a part that is your favorite. That would be your favorite scene. To report on your book, you will be sharing your favorite scene. But instead of just telling someone, you will be sharing it with many people in a dramatic form, just like a play. You may share your favorite scene in a monologue, a dialogue, or a puppet show.

The Monologue: A monologue is dialogue with just one person. Sometimes actors are on stage all alone, and they talk to themselves (admit it, you do it too, occasionally). Ask your teacher to find a monologue written by Shakespeare; he wrote many famous ones. If your favorite scene has a character struggling with a decision or trying to figure something out all by himself, you will be doing a monologue. Practice it several times until you are feeling so comfortable with the words that you are beginning to act and feel the emotions of the scene. Add your props and costume, if you wish, and you are ready to perform.

Dialogue: You have probably guessed by now that a dialogue is a conversation between two or more people. If your favorite scene has two or more people saying things to each other, you will be sharing a dialogue. You and a friend or two will need to get together to rehearse your scene. You will each need a script in the beginning, but you should have your lines memorized before you perform. Practice until you all know what to do and can speak your lines with expression. If you wish, you can add props and costumes.

Puppet Show: You may prefer to stay behind the scenes and make others speak the lines. With a puppet show you can do just that. There are many ways you can do this. You can make papier-mâché heads (be sure to poke a finger hole) and, with your hand inside an old sock, stick them on top of your fingers. You can use old socks and decorate them with fabric, felt, markers, etc., or you can draw the characters on cardboard, color them, and glue them to craft sticks to make stick puppets. These are simple ways. You can use your imagination and make almost any kind of puppet you want. You will still need to present your scene after practicing the lines. But you can tape the lines behind the stage so you can read them with expression. For a puppet stage, you can use a large cardboard box (see if you can find an appliance box) and cut a rectangle out of the front of it. Decorate the box to look like a fancy stage, or you can even drape old sheets around two chairs to create a stage.

My Favorite Scene *(cont.)*

Examples of a monologue and a dialogue:

Monologue

Jake: (*walks into the house, starts to slam the door, and then changes mind and shuts it firmly*) Anyone home? No one's home. Figures. I have the most frustrating, most horrible day of my life and there is no one here to comfort me. Not a soul. (*opens refrigerator, rummages about, closes it and walks over and flops on couch*) Not a soul. I am totally alone in this world. First I am rejected by Coach Miller, then by Leticia Juarez. Then I drop my science notebook and all my papers go into the gutter. I quit. I quit everything! (*stands and waves arms about for emphasis*) I quit soccer! I quit having anything to do with girls! I quit science! I . . . (lowers arms) . . . I'm hungry! (*goes back to refrigerator but is interrupted by ringing telephone; runs to answer it*) Hellooooo!??? (*speaks cheerfully*)

Dialogue

Hector: (*hurries to catch up to Jake*) Jake! Did you find all your science papers?

Jake: Are you kidding? They were all ruined! The gutter was full of this yucky, muddy slime!

Hector: I know someone who wants to let you borrow some very complete science papers.

Jake: (*they are nearing front of school*) Forget it, Hector, yours are not that great, and I can't afford them anyway.

Hector: (*runs off*) Shows how little you know! I'm not going to tell you now!

Jake: (*stops walking*) Hector? Hector! Who? Please come back . . .

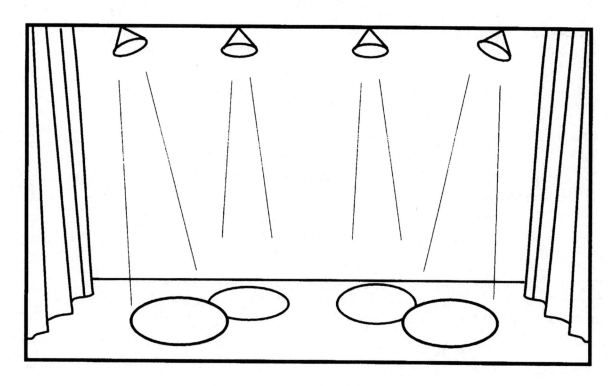

All About the Setting

You have read a play. Where does it take place? In a jungle land? In a desert? In a foreign country? On the sea?

Let's take the example of a foreign country. If your play takes place in a foreign country, how much do you know about this country? Make a list of what you already know. When you have finished that, make a list of what you would like to know. Now, be an investigator and find out all you can about the country. You can research at the library, at home, at school, in the newspaper, in magazines, encyclopedias (printed volumes and computer); there are so many places to find information. Look for information you want to know and more.

When you have collected your information, you can present it in several different ways:

- You can create a table display with information, pictures and posters, objects, and your list of things you knew, wanted to know, and discovered.

- You can learn some of the language of that foreign country and teach a language lesson to the class.

- You can write an illustrated report and put it into a binder to share with the class.

- You can create a video about the country and include all you learned.

- You can take the class on a travelogue. Share pictures, slides, and stories with the class.

- You can research the food of that foreign country and bring in samples to share with the class.

- You can bring in samples of the music from that setting and let the class listen.

- You can research the history of that setting and create a time line.

- If the playwright grew up in the setting, you can find out about what his life was like while he was growing up in that setting. Share it with the class.

- You can send for travel brochures about the setting and create a display the class can look at.

Maybe you have some ideas of your own, too, about how to report on the setting of your play. Whatever you choose to do, be sure that you include information about the play itself and what is important about the play taking place in this setting.

42

A Collage

You have probably made a collage before, but have you ever made a collage about a play? It's not important for you to find pictures of your play. The idea is to create a collage of your impressions of the play. It's always a good idea to brainstorm before a new project, so brainstorm some lists of impressions from the play you read. Here is a list of examples.

colors

sounds

textures (sandy, watery, rough, grassy, rocky)

smells

appearances (How were the characters dressed?)

words (a word that a character often repeated or a word that comes to mind when you think of the play)

foods (Do the characters eat certain foods, or is preparing a particular meal a central part of a scene?)

setting (mountains, city, seaport, village, suburban home)

culture (Is there a particular culture represented?)

Is there anything else that you have thought of?

Keep your list nearby as you look through old magazines and other publications. When you see something that you might be able to use, tear it out. Soon you will have more than you can use, even though it will seem like you don't have enough. That's when it is time to create your collage. Tear and cut the items you think you can use (remember you can write words by finding them already spelled for you, for example, "cinnamon" to represent a smell; you can spell the word yourself by cutting the letters individually from different sources—don't worry; they don't need to all look alike).

Arrange the pictures, colors, letters, textures, etc. on a medium or large piece of cardboard or poster board. Try different images and different arrangements until you find what you like. When you know what you like, start gluing the images into place.

Now fill in the form below, attach it to the back of your collage, and bring it to class. You may not be able to use each of these categories, but you should be able to use at least four or five of them.

Name _____

Title of Play _____ Author _____

I chose the following colors _____ to represent_____

The sounds of the play _____ are represented by_____

The following textures _____ represent _____

The smells _____ of the play are represented by _____

The following items _____ represent the characters and their appearance because _____

I have added the following word(s) _____ because_____

The foods I have chosen _____ represent_____

I have shown the culture of the play's setting with _____

I have also used the following pictures or words _____ because _____

Setting the Scene

By the time that a play is being presented on stage, a set designer has already been at work creating what the play will look like from the backdrop (what you see in the background whether it is rolling hills, a city scene, or a family living room) to the props (furniture, light poles, weeds, whatever the scene calls for) to the actors and what they will look like in the scene, where they will be, etc.

This is your chance to create a book report about the play you read by being a set designer.

For your stage set diorama you will need the following:

- a shoe box
- construction paper or shelf paper
- lightweight tagboard
- scissors
- glue
- tape
- crayons or markers
- optional:
  magazine pictures
  adhesive paper to cover the outside of the box

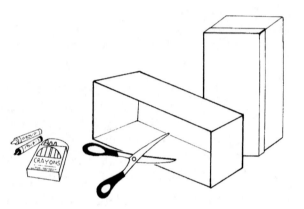

Directions:

1. Take off the cover of the shoe box.

2. Cover the outside, if you wish, or glue on construction paper "curtains," or create the outside of the theater, complete with a marquee (a sign showing what is playing, which would be the title of your play, of course).

3. To make a pattern for the inner walls, lay the box on the construction paper and measure the size of the three outer sides. Fold the paper around the box and cut around the outline.

4. Decorate the inner walls with drawings, magazine pictures, or paint to represent the scene's backdrop.

5. Glue the walls in place inside the box.

6. Cover the stage floor in the same way. If you can get some "wood-grained" adhesive paper, you might want to use that so it looks like the wood floor of a stage.

7. Tagboard and construction paper may be used to make other free-standing pictures for the scene. Create trees, buildings, furniture, props, and even actors and actresses. You might want to think of lots of different materials to use in creating the objects in your scene, such as foil, cotton balls, fabric, yarn, glitter, string, clay, twigs, toothpicks, grass clippings, straw flowers, ribbons, matchboxes (painted).

8. Label the outside with the name of the play and the playwright (the marquee would be perfect for this!) and your name.

9. Write a page to tell about the book and the particular scene that is being presented on stage.

Having a Character Day

A character day can be simple or complex, depending upon what you want to make it and what your time and resources are like. If it is the culminating activity at the end of a year of a love affair with new fictional books, you may want it to be complex enough to cap off the year. If it is an end-of-the-week activity, you may want it to be more simple. Here are some ideas that range from the simple to the complex to add to your own good ideas.

A Character Clue Day can be planned for which each child brings an object related to a book character. The class tries to guess the character. For example, a shiny, silver shoe could lead to Dorothy from *The Wizard of Oz.*

Model Characters can be created and interviewed as favorite book characters are turned into life-sized paper dolls. Have the students work in pairs. One child lies on a large sheet of paper while the partner traces his or her outline. Then each child colors his outline to look not like him or herself but like the character in the book. One at a time, the models can be "seated" in a chair before the class and interviewed by the students. The "creator" can give the answers to the questions. Afterwards, the characters can be posted around the room with dialogue balloons. Have your students write a quote from the character in a dialogue balloon and add these to each character on display.

A Character Day can be accomplished by any of the above or the suggested activity on page 19 wherein the students, one at a time, come to class as the character of their book. Also, you can hold a character day as a kind of whole class celebration. In this case, have each student come to class as the character on the chosen day. Be sure to notify parents well in advance so they can assist in preparing "costumes" and/or props. Remind parents that there is no need to go out and purchase a ready-made costume. It is best to discourage this and, instead, encourage students to be creative and create costumes from items found on hand. When you notify parents, also ask that they see if there are any foods mentioned in the book their child read; if so, see if they can send some of that food to the celebration, labeled with the kind of food it is and the title of the book. If there is no food included in the book, parents can send related foods according to the setting and culture of the book. Create a form that can be returned so you can coordinate all efforts and know how many visitors you can expect. If you prefer, you might want to research a little and send out a list of "Storybook Foods" (foods mentioned in nursery rhymes and popular children's books). Have parents sign up for foods they will make and, if possible, send the recipes home.

Fairy Tale Foods

Please send one of the following foods:

1. Porridge (*The Three Bears*)

2. Gingerbread Cookies (*The Gingerbread Boy*)

3. _____

Having a Character Day *(cont.)*

Have students create placemats that match the theme and the character of the book they read (one for themselves and one for each family member who will attend). Paper cups, plates, and napkins can be many colors if you can't find a "bookish" theme.

A week before, have your students create an invitation that will go to their families. Be sure their invitations are "in character." Have them sign their invitations as the characters they will be representing.

On character day, each child will come to school as the character of the book he or she read. You may play a guessing game to have guests try to figure out who they are (add clues if it is not easy to guess from the "costume"; some may be dressed as "normal people" if that is appropriate for their characters). Be sure each character is introduced and interviewed briefly. Also, be sure that the food is "introduced" and connections made to the literature. If the students brought food representing their books, have them introduce and explain the dishes they brought.

Keeping a Notebook of Book Reviews

There are several ways to organize student book reviews. If it is an activity that you do once or twice a year, one thick notebook may suffice. You can organize it according to genres or book titles. Once or twice during the school year, each student should write a book review. You may wish to create a form for this and then students can fill it in (see below) and add an illustration to the back.

If you will be handling many book reviews, you may wish to have a separate notebook for each genre and then perhaps dividers for specific books.

Another way to keep book reviews would be in file boxes. Student book reviews could be written on index cards and filed according to genres, authors, or titles.

The book review notebooks or files are useful on many levels.

One way they are useful is in giving students the opportunity to quickly respond to a book they have read, giving their opinion of it.

Besides the writing and reading comprehension aspects of this activity, it is also a means of making a book report.

Depending on how you decide to organize the book reviews, they can be an asset in teaching your students various organizational skills. Give them opportunities to file their reviews according to the filing system you are using. Alphabetizing book reviews according to title or author (or both, if you choose to have duplicate copies of reviews) is good practice for students who will need to feel at ease researching by using dictionaries, library filing systems, encyclopedias, and computer research software.

In addition, students can look through the notebooks to see what other students thought of a particular book. This can encourage a student to try a book he or she ordinarily might not have chosen. If you can keep notebooks for all the years you teach, your current students can benefit from the wisdom of many students who have gone before.

Another advantage of the book review notebook is that students can see that there are differing opinions on various books and that this is okay. Their opinions are as valid as those of other students. This will aid in the development of self-esteem.

My Book Review

Name _____

Title of Book _____

Name of Author _____

Do you like this book? _____

_____

Who is your favorite character? _____

What part do you like the best? (Don't give away the ending!) _____

_____

Do you think your friends would like to read this book? _____

_____

How many smiles would you give this book? Color them in.

Literature Journals

A literature journal is a notebook that students keep while they are reading a particular book. There are many ways to keep a literature journal, and you may have your students do one or all of the following or have additional ideas to modify an idea below. The following steps are written to your students, so you may copy the rest of the page and give one to each student, perhaps inside the cover of a blank notebook, or choose which ideas you like best and combine them with your own as you introduce your students to literature journals.

✎ Using a notebook, write your name, the name of the book, and its author on the cover.

✎ Inside, you will need to use a ruler to draw a line down the middle of each page. Each page will be divided in half lengthwise.

✎ After you read, you write the date at the top of the page and the page numbers you read.

✎ Then, in the left-hand column you write a quote, a scene, a bit of dialogue, or a description from the book that you especially liked or found especially interesting.

✎ In the right-hand column, write your response to what you wrote in the left-hand column. Why do you like that quote, dialogue, or description? What does it remind you of? Does it inspire you to write something of your own? Does it inspire you to think of someone, do something good, or tell someone something? Does it make you think? Does it make you feel happy, sad, angry, or some other feeling? Do you like something about how the author wrote it? Write anything you can think of.

✎ Leave a space at the bottom of the page for your teacher to respond to your writing.

✎ Don't worry; this is not a time when he or she will be checking your grammar and spelling. It's just a time to enjoy your response to the literature and an opportunity for your teacher to also respond. You'll probably enjoy it as you get further into the book. It will be like having someone else reading with you.

✎ When you have finished the book, you will have a notebook full of your thoughts and ideas and favorite parts of the book. And you will have a good book report all ready to turn in.

✎ If there is room on your pages, you can draw a picture of something from the book to go with what you wrote.

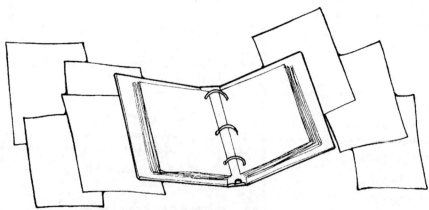